a merchant seaman talks

My Name is Frank

Frank Laskier

Solis Press

ALSO BY FRANK LASKIER
AND AVAILABLE FROM SOLIS PRESS:
Log Book
Unseen Harbour

Originally published in 1941 by George Allen & Unwin, London. This edition completely reset and published in 2021 by Solis Press

Caution: please be aware that some of the language used is of its time and today is considered inappropriate.

Typographical arrangement, annotations, introduction and appendix copyright © 2021 Solis Press

Footnotes added by the publisher for this new edition are indicated by the use of square brackets.

Images: cover is based on the original jacket design of the 1941 edition. p. 72: National Archives.

All rights reserved. No part of this publication may be reproduced, stored in a retrieval system, or transmitted, in any form or by any means, electronic, mechanical, photocopying, recording or otherwise, except as permitted by the UK Copyright, Designs and Patents Act 1988, without the prior permission of the publisher.

This book is sold subject to the condition that it shall not, by way or trade or otherwise, be lent, resold, hired out or otherwise circulated without the publisher's prior consent in any form of binding or cover other than in which it is published and without a similar condition including this condition being imposed on the subsequent purchaser.

ISBN: 978-1-910146-47-7

Published by Solis Press, Tunbridge Wells, Kent, England

Web: www.solispress.com | *Twitter*: @SolisPress

Contents

Introduction to this new edition 5

Foreword 9

1. Why I am a Sailor 15

2. Joining your Ship 18

3. Bananas 20

4. Nick Tamlin 24

5. *British Corporal* 27

6. Talk to Seamen, Liverpool 30

7. Forty-three Days in an Open Boat 33

8. Tough Mate 35

9. The Dive Bomber 37

10. *City of Benares, San Demetrio, Eurylochus* . . . 39

11. On a Raft 47

12. Meeting the Navy 50

13. Sea Raider 52

14. Sister Morris 55

15. My Street 57

Postscript 60

Appendix: Details of the vessels mentioned . . 61

FRANK LASKIER 1912–1949

Introduction to this new edition

In 1941, an unknown, unnamed merchant seaman gave a series of radio talks. In these, he described in graphic and terrifying detail what it was like to serve on the convoys bringing vital supplies across the oceans into Britain during the Second World War.

The talks came about when a BBC radio journalist investigating the bombing in British ports visited the Liverpool Sailors' House. While there, the journalist overheard a man recounting how his ship had been torpedoed by the German navy and of his miraculous rescue despite terrible injuries. It was such a compelling story, raw and full of rage, that the journalist persuaded the man to give a short broadcast so that the people at home could understand the perils faced by those who risked, and sometimes gave, their lives to provide food and other essential materials for the nation.

Listeners of the radio broadcast, which was given without a script or rehearsal, were astounded to hear the voice of an ordinary man describing the horrific realities of the war at sea. The huge popular response resulted in the sailor being asked to give further talks on his experiences and, before long, the identity of the unknown seaman was revealed: his name was Frank Laskier. Laskier was born in 1912 in the suburbs of Liverpool and had run away to join the merchant navy while a young teenager.

After giving the talks, and despite the loss of his left foot, Laskier himself signed up for another ship, as documented in the government-sponsored film *Seaman Frank Goes Back to Sea* (1942).

Laskier's radio talks are transcribed in this book, which was first published in 1941. The book reviewer of *The Spectator* said:

> Frank Laskier's broadcasts had the stuff of greatness; put into print they lose nothing in the reading. By a natural genius this seaman has found an expression and a rhythm which the poets and artists of the modern world have been striving after for generations.

My Name is Frank was followed up in 1942 with a new work by Laskier entitled *Log Book* (also reissued by Solis Press in 2021). Although *Log Book* was described as fiction, it is, in fact, a thinly veiled no-holes-barred autobiography detailing Laskier's own, often wild, life at sea.

Among those impressed by Laskier was a newspaper journalist who wrote in 1942:

> Here was a humble man without money or schooling. Yet he spoke the tongue that Shakespeare spoke. His voice was soft, but inescapable. He knew Shakespeare, and could interweave Shakespeare's phrases with his story so that they sounded as if they were spun that very moment. Nothing was unintelligible or out of date or strange about them; as he used them, they were better than new. When he spoke you could hear the waves thud and smash against the sides, feel the ship lurch and stagger as the torpedo struck, see the men, with strained faces and blowing hair, toiling to get the boats out. He minted his own phrases, too, and they came out shining gold. A bomb bit the ship and made a noise 'like the opening of the gates of hell'. It made 'a bloody gruel of men's bodies'. One man fell into a boat and lay there 'with a face like a bucketful of ashes'; his mates did not know, till he died, that his ribs were all stove in. (From Douglas Reed, *All Our To-morrows*, Jonathan Cape, 1942, pp. 120–30.)

Perhaps today we might be dismissive of heroic tales from the Second World War, suggesting that they are merely propaganda pieces. But it is important to remember that this was an authentic voice of an ordinary man – not a historian, a politician, or a great admiral – but an ordinary man doing his bit for his country.

After the war, Laskier settled in the USA with his wife. There he continued to write, publishing short stories in *Esquire* and *Collier's* magazines. He also wrote a novel, an adventure story entitled *Unseen Harbour* which was published in 1947 and has also been reissued by Solis Press in 2021. Sadly, Laskier's literary career was cut short as he was killed in a car accident in New York City in 1949.

A note on the text

This reissued edition of *My Name is Frank* has had some small amendments made to the text, for example where words were repeated or omitted.

The publisher has added some explanatory footnotes for this new edition. These are differentiated from the author's own by using square brackets. The publisher has also added an appendix (pages 61–71) listing the ships mentioned in the book along with brief descriptions.

Foreword
by Eldon Moore[1]

THIS BOOK IS PROBABLY unique, since it has never been written. Every word has been spoken to the microphone by a merchant seaman, who talked without so much as a rehearsal or a note in front of him.

It takes its title from the opening words of the tenth talk here, which was one of the first he actually recorded. Frank did not wish his surname to be known, since he regards himself as no more than a representative of his mates, the seamen of the Merchant Navy. The Press, however, has stripped him of his anonymity.

When he first spoke in the BBC's Home Service,[2] a woman wrote in to say that it was the finest talk she had heard since the outbreak of war. It was so good that she felt sure it must be "phoney". Quite a lot of other people have implied their belief that Frank's broadcasts were prepared by a skilled writer and spoken by a first-class actor. I hope this book will finally dispel any lingering doubts about Frank's authenticity.

This is how he came to the BBC microphone. In the late spring of 1941 Terence de Marney, an "Observer"—radio equivalent of newspaper reporter—went on a tour of some of the badly bombed British ports, taking a recording car and engineer with him. I was one of the party, since such an expedition was likely to provide good material for articles, especially for the listeners to the BBC's Empire Service.

Among the places we visited was the Seamen's Home at Liverpool. Our time-table would not allow us more than an afternoon to gather records and copy. But we agreed that it

---
1 [Moore worked for BBC radio and wrote this foreword for the 1941 edition.]
2 [A radio station that broadcast from 1939 to 1967, when it was replaced by Radio 4.]

was a promising place for first-class material, since seamen fetch up there straight from the Battle of the Atlantic,[3] many of them the survivors of torpedoed ships.

So a little later de Marney got leave to return to Liverpool, where he spent six weeks as an ordinary inmate of the Home, living, sleeping, eating, drinking with its shifting population, becoming so much their mate, so much part of the furniture, that they lost all self-consciousness in his presence and talked as men do only when they feel at ease among friends.

He heard many good stories, naturally, but not the ace story and the ace speaker that he felt sure would turn up in the long run.

After some weeks he got wind of a seaman with "a bee in his bonnet" about using petrol for joy-rides. That was Frank, and de Marney found him perfectly ready to talk. He had only to hear him once to know that he had found what he was looking for. He phoned for a recording car, set the microphone down in front of Frank at a table in a Liverpool café, and said, "Now then, Frank, when you're ready, tell me that story again".

That story is told in the tenth talk here, the story of the *San Demetrio*, which had a friend of Frank's aboard her.

The remarkable thing about that broadcast is that it happened precisely as I have said. Without a script or a note, without a hesitation, Frank told the microphone his story exactly as it is printed here. The same happened with every other talk. De Marney, living in Frank's pocket all the time, would simply let him yarn until some fresh treasure came floating up from the depths of Frank's photographic memory. Then de Marney would say, "That's the story I want", arrange for a recording as soon as possible, and sit Frank down in front of the microphone again. Very often what

---

3 [The longest campaign of the Second World War, which ran from 1939 to Germany's defeat in 1945. At its core was the Allied naval blockade of Germany and Germany's subsequent counter-blockade.]

he said then was not quite the same as the first version, for he would be re-thinking and re-remembering again as he talked to the microphone.

The talks as printed here are simply the verbatim reports of the recordings. All I have done is to arrange them in an order that will give a consecutive picture of Frank's experiences, and to punctuate them. The last has been my greatest difficulty. It may be possible to punctuate and paragraph a prepared platform speech according to the canons of the printed word. But it is quite impossible to make those canons give a true interpretation of the speech of a man who is thinking aloud, whispering to himself rather than to the microphone.

So I have set those canons aside, and punctuated in a way that would be anathema to the literary stylist, using dashes as often as not instead of stops, "and" to begin a sentence, making paragraphs, sometimes, of single short sentences. If the method is wrong, the fault is solely mine. But it seems to give a truer picture than the conventional method could of the unrehearsed drama as Frank's memories come welling up to catch him by the throat.

Occasionally, but not always, I have cut out a few words where Frank has stumbled or repeated himself. I have inserted a few explanatory notes.[4]

Otherwise this book is Frank's and Frank's alone, just as he first spoke it, speaking so low that the microphone had to be pressed up a few inches from his lips. That helps to account, by the way, for the rare emotional quality of his words as they come out of the loudspeaker. Most people speak fairly loudly, and the microphone is a foot or more away. But it is so close to Frank that it picks up his very breathing and the swift catch of breath as an old memory grips him again.

---

4 [The word "*query*" has been inserted in the original text. Presumably this is where the Eldon failed to understand a word, or it may have been censored.]

He had another considerable advantage. He was recording, not going out "live". So he had not to bother about timing. A third advantage was actually that he spoke without a script. Most people tend to talk too fast for the microphone, and to become unnatural if they slow down. But Frank, digging down into his memory and thinking aloud, speaks naturally at the right speed, and also with those natural pauses, accelerations and slowings down of speech which prevent monotony.

But those are minor points. The chief reason for Frank's success, I think, is simply that he is a seaman. There are many thousands of seamen who have had like experiences, and of them some hundreds, probably, share Frank's natural taste and gift of yarning. In the peaceful, monotonous life of the peace-time sailor, as described in the first talk here, such men are valued shipmates and one yarn will set another going. Also, men who are not constantly reading and writing tend to have better memories than office folk, and their vivid experiences bite deep.

But these other Franks have not yet been discovered.

There is no need, either, to be surprised at Frank's occasional flashing phrase, or his obvious acquaintance with some of the classics of English literature. The vivid phrase comes naturally to the lips of men who have vivid experiences; and many seamen are much better read than their fellows ashore. The sea gives a lot of time to be killed by reading, and every ship's library contains, besides (Frank's words) "a lot of trash", the Bible and Shakespeare at least, and often a lot more of the nobler stuff of our tongue. Also a seaman's language is not daily vitiated by the clichés of the daily Press.

Frank, who was avid for books as a boy, has since read Kipling, Conrad, and Stevenson—and probably others that I have not yet heard him mention. This explains a good deal in a man with a photographic memory.

I have tried to show that Frank is only typical of his fellow seamen. It is what he would like me to do; and I believe it is also the truth. I have sailed in the little ships and feel I know the breed who man them. I only need to sketch Frank's own personality and background, which seem equally typical.

His father, also a seaman until he retired to a ship's laundry business, had ten children whom he ruled with a tongue of iron—ruled, that is until each one in turn showed the old man's own determination to go their own ways. Then he forgave them; and the family, though bad letter-writers and scattered all over the globe, is still a united family. Frank describes himself as the black sheep because he has never, like the others, risen in the world. He is still a deckhand owing to "mental laziness" and dislike of mathematics. Another reason, I think, is that he does not want executive responsibility and loves the carefree life and comradeship of the ordinary seaman.

For some generations the family has been rooted in Wallasey, Cheshire, where Frank spent a happy boyhood. At the age of sixteen he had "a blazing row" with his father because he refused to read for the Ministry. A little later, when he had delivered the laundry to a ship and collected the money, a head looked over the side of another ship and said, "Come to America, sonnie?" Frank scrambled up, and half an hour later was on his way across the Atlantic as the "Peggy" (boy) with 5s. 6d.[5] of his father's money.

It was several months before his family even knew what had happened to him.

Ever since then Frank has followed the sea. He is now twenty-nine, but looks nearer forty. That is quite usual among seamen. In shore-going kit he does not look like a seaman. But that also is usual. He is about 5 feet 10 inches tall, of the lean and narrow build, dark and already going thin on top.

---

5 [Five shillings and sixpence. In modern currency this is 27.5p. The equivalent of about £12 nowadays.]

He is a most entertaining companion, quick in the conversational come-back, and enjoying his yarning as much as his hearers. He is a little more grown up than most of his mates whom I once described as being like "delightful children" when ashore. "No!" he corrected me, "adolescents". I still do not agree with him; while I found that taking Frank himself round London was like taking the nicest possible nephew to his first pantomime.

In one respect, however, Frank, like his fellows, is no longer childlike. The Germans have taught him, as his later talks show, the holy gift of hatred.

1. Why I am a Sailor

PARTICULARLY IN WARTIME WHEN we're suffering such damage, and going through such an exciting period in our lives, a lot of people have asked me why I am a sailor— "Why don't I get a shore job, or why don't I do anything to get out of this?"—as it seems a pretty suicide sort of job according to them.

But the whole thing goes a lot deeper than that. I'll tell you my ideas on the subject.

You remember that depression affair in 1934 and 1935 and 1936—around that time? Well, we were going away to sea then, I in particular was going away. And I'd come on shore and seen people weren't so very, very happy. But, somehow or other, all that happened to you shore-side people— don't think I'm speaking contemptuously, because I mean I have a great respect for people on shore—but everything that happened on shore seemed to us to be unreal, somehow or other.

It was peacetime, we could go ashore, we could get our drink, do our shopping, see our wives, or sweethearts, or our parents, and then go away to sea.

And there is something definitely different about going away to sea, which has got me since I first pushed off, when I was about sixteen.

It's that frame of mind that you get into when you are on a long trip. Say you're going in between Abadan[6] and Australia, beating down on the south-east trades,[7] and you see the sun rising every morning in the same spot. The same sea, the same sky, and the same fresh glorious breeze. The same peace and contentment. Then you can get all your

---

6 [A port in modern-day Iran. It has a large oil refinery.]
7 [The trade winds are prevailing winds in the equatorial region, they are north-easterly in the northern hemisphere and south-easterly in the southern hemisphere.]

dhobying[8] out, and you can wash and scrub your clothes, and rinse them out, and compare notes—and we're much more finicky than any housewife could ever be.

And you get hold of a piece of spun yarn, and you put your clothes on it, and you hang them up on the poop.

And you have the beautiful, continuous, and easy watch and watch—4 to 8, 4 to 8, 4 to 8.[9]

You get your meals and you're happy. You don't have to bother about cigarettes. You can sit out on the poop at night in the dog watches,[10] and yarn and yarn—and we *always* talk about ships. And somehow or other a peace gets into your soul. Otherwise, why do we go back to sea?

When we join a ship, we continually howl and groan; and we always say that the last ship is the best ship. But it isn't true. Every ship is the best ship. Every ship when you have your mates with you, and you know your skipper. *You* may see her on the horizon, a dirty little frowsy tramp—so she looks. But you haven't seen our quarters; you haven't met our friends. You haven't tasted the sweetness of coffee at twelve o'clock at night.

You haven't listened to the thrill of the striking of sixteen bells on New Year's Eve. You haven't sailed up the river to your home port, and you haven't joined her.

We are a race apart. We are the sailors.

And do you think that a nation like the Germans could ever drive us from the sea? Do you think that a dive bomber could stop us from earning our livelihood? Do you think they would ever deprive us of the only peace we have ever known on earth?

---

8 [A *dhobi* is an Indian term for someone who washes clothes.]
9 [On a merchant ship, watchkeepers often keep watch for six periods of four consecutive hours: so Frank is referring to 0400–0800 and 1600–2000 watches which would be worked on a three-day rota.]
10 [Where a regular watch period would be reduced to help rotate the crew members.]

Frank Laskier

We are British, we are they who go down to the sea in ships, and occupy their business in big waters. We see the glory of the Lord—and we *do*. And we always will, and that is why we are sailors.

2. Joining your Ship

WE HAVE A SAYING in the Merchant Service, "If you've signed your ship, you've got to join her"; and it has a lot of equivalents in shore life—such a saying as "a man is as good as his word", and things like that. But it just means that amongst we who follow the sea for a living, that once you have put your pen to paper and signed your name then, no matter what happens, you must join your ship.

You walk out of the shipping office and in your pocket you have two pieces of paper. One is an allotment note for some money to be stopped out of your wages, to give to your wife or your mother each week, and the other is an advance note. The advance note is a sort of sub[11] on your wages. Well, you take your advance note round, and there are several sharks who are always waiting to cash them for you; and sometimes they're not sharks, they're darn nice people, and you get the money from them. They usually charge you about sixpence in the pound—the nice people I mean—and then you go off.

You may have one or two drinks—it just depends how you feel like it—but there on your advance note and your allotment paper is written, "You will join your ship at five minutes past twelve, evening", or "at night". You go out and you buy your soap. Have you ever seen a sailor buying soap? He isn't put off by any cheap substitute; it must be good soap. You buy your soap and your soap flakes—maybe if you're feeling very, very finicky indeed, a couple of packets of patent soap powder.

And you buy matches by the gross; you buy razor blades by the dozen, and you always forget *something*. Usually you forget to buy a toothbrush, or toothpaste. That means you've either got to clean your teeth with a towel or with a brush and some soap. Both of them are pretty horrible alternatives.

---

11 [An advance payment on promised wages.]

Frank Laskier

You pack all these things into your pocket and you stand there at about nine o'clock at night and you think, "Well, have I got everything?"—Believe me, no housewife ever living has such a worry. But we don't let it worry us too much and then we go home.

And then there is that horrible moment that always hurts—it's always hurt me I know—when you get up out of your easy-chair at about half-past ten, and the last bus is going and the ship is waiting. And being a man and a sailor, you can't kiss people good-bye; and you sort of look at each other and shake hands and say, "Well, I'll be seeing you". And with a heart that's always heavy you set off for your ship.

And you come on board, climbing up the gangway with your kit bag on your shoulder, and you make your way aft or for'ard to your quarters and you dump your things down. And never has the fo'c'sle[12] looked more dirty or more gloomy or more small; and you go on gangway watch.

And the next morning you are out about five in the morning, breaking out the anchor—and away you go downstream, and your heart is always heavy with misery at the thought of leaving your friends behind.

And then about the second day out something happens to you. Maybe you're coming down from the wheel, maybe stiff with cold. You just crawl out of the foretop-lookout, the crow's nest, and you're coming down the shrouds; and you get on to the for'ard well-deck, and you shake yourself in your oilskins and your sea boots.

And you trudge along the deck with that inimitable walk that all good sailors have, and you pass the galley and you see the old cook there and you shout out, "Hullo Doc, what's for dinner?"—and maybe he shouts out "bacon and eggs", *maybe*. But you're hungry, you're young, you're helpless. You're holding down a man's job, and you've joined your ship.

---

12 [The forward part of a ship. Originally called the forecastle and *foksle* represents the usual pronunciation.]

3. Bananas

Do you remember in the piping time of peace, those long, smooth, yellow objects, with the hard, thick, tough skin outside, and very nice and soft and sweet inside? They had a sort of gentle curve to them, what were they called?— Oh yes, bananas.[13]

Well, you remember in those idle days, when we used to have our bananas and cream and things like that? Did you ever wonder how we did bring them over?

The old banana boats, they're quite a tradition in their way, because men who sail with them never sail in any other. You go out to the West Indies to pick up your bananas, or you can go right out to the West Coast of Africa. Well, the West Coast trip isn't too good. But out at Trinidad and Jamaica, Port Arthur, Port of Spain, Montego Bay, Port Anthony, Santa Marta—my word, what a heavenly time we used to have there!

The decks were always absolutely spotlessly white with the long black lines of the pitch running between the planks; ship painted white; everybody spotlessly clean. And finally we would receive orders, after tootling in and out of all those funny little ports, in the back of beyond. Then we would call in at Montego Bay and finish loading cargoes.

You get into Montego Bay, and there's a little island on the port bow as you get in, and you pass the island and round into a perfect little landlocked harbour. And there all that you ever hear is the rattle of the anchor, as she's broke out, and drops. All you hear is the roar of the chain as she is brought up, and you depart. For the rest you have silence.

---

13 [Although this is perhaps the most common fruit consumed in Britain today, it was rationed during the Second World War. Deliveries did not resume until after the war had ended.]

Frank Laskier

And the night comes in about twenty minutes and the ship is there, and they take out lights and put them over the side and open the doors in the ship's side. And you gaze in at that beautiful translucent circle of green, and see funny little fishes swimming round underneath, and you're talking there idly with your shipmates, waiting for the bananas on board. You're anchored out in the Bay of course, and you flick your cigarette ash and you watch that tiny little spot of ash as it circles and floats down and is lost in the water. You can see the dim haze of the mountains in the distance, and the sparkle of lights from the loading jetty. And you hear a dull murmur from the shore, that gets louder and louder and louder, of men singing, arguing, and shouting.

And then into that magic circle of light there comes an enormous great scow,[14] and it is absolutely packed with humanity—large, brawny West Indians. And they come alongside with torrents of language and terrific flat spins of arguments and shouts and screams. And they pour on board like a constant stream, and you hear them as they scream their heads off down below in the holds.

And then again into the magic circle of light there appear four even bigger scows, with a large and solitary man with a long pole at the stern end; and he sculls her gently round in the water and ties her underneath the stage. Then you see something ... I'll never forget it—I'll never forget the first man I saw doing that particular stunt.

He was there on a tiny little cat-walk stretched across the gunwale of the boat of this scow, and there was a man port and starboard on the for'ard end and port and starboard on the aft—you know, one on each corner of the boat. And he was there, an enormous man about, oh! six foot, great brawny brown shoulders, a pair of very, very baggy trousers, a large sun hat even though it was dark, and he's saying now, "Come on, boys, we's going to load this ship. Now come on."

---
14 [A small flat-bottomed barge.]

And then I saw something that I've never seen equalled yet. Every man in every corner bent down and seized up a huge bunch of bananas—they weigh about a hundredweight[15]—lifted it over his head, slung it at the talkative laddie on the cat-walk, and he seized each bunch like a streak of lightning, dancing round there on the board.

Each bunch was grabbed up with a heave right on to the stage into the ship—and again, and again, and again. And he never stopped talking and he never stopped working.

He had to bend down as the load got lower, and as it got farther for'ard, or farther aft, the men had to throw farther. But they were coming there from each corner one, two, three, four, one hundredweight at a time, long bunches of bananas on a stalk and he'd seize them—smack, and you could hear them hitting his hands. And you could see the ripples of the muscles under his shoulders, as he hurled them up into the air and on to the stage.

There were four doors on the ship's side port, four doors on the ship's side for'ard. Those men were loading the whole time. The noise was indescribable. And they loaded that ship, or completed the loading, in twelve hours. And then they departed the way they had come.

The next morning we had to wait for mail or something, and I got a boat on shore. Just there on that little jetty I crawled up the green, slimy ladder and along there, with the ground all littered with banana skins and large spiders stalking relentlessly about, and then on to the beach. Underneath the little huts there I found my large friend of the night before, our large, talkative athlete. And I sat down by him, offered him a cigarette, and asked him how he was getting on, and he turned round to me with eyes that were glazed with the inherited sloth of centuries of idle living.

He said, "Well boss, you see, we work things like this. We never see anything round here for months, and months, and

---

15 [Eight stone or approximately 51 kg.]

weeks, and weeks. Well, a boy wants to play a little bit dice occasionally, he wants to get a drink of rum occasionally, so when the boat comes in we just loads up the skins and we work for about twelve hours"—and his voice died away to idleness and sleep.

That is the way they were living—twelve hours' work, six months' idleness. And if I'd had any sense at all I think I'd have stayed there and loaded bananas with him for the rest of my life. Really, I wanted to.

4. Nick Tamlin

(In this talk Frank was clearly addressing his fellow seamen)

ABOUT FIVE YEARS AGO I was down in my home in the *query*[16] village—and I don't mean Barry Docks, I mean Falmouth—and there I met a man, the most amazing, the most astounding person I've ever met in all my life. His name was Nick Tamlin, and he was bo'sun of one of the British tankers. You could say that he was tough, but he was more than tough. He had an air of restrained violence about him. He knew things; he had sailed.

When the war started in Spain[17] he was one of the first to sign up with that Greek who was running ships out there, and go down to Valencia.[18] He had his first taste of warfare, of modern warfare, from the Germans and the Italians running ships between Valencia and Alicante.[19]

Nick Tamlin! You have to see him to believe him. A tall man, red-faced, blue eyes, never under any circumstances wearing anything like ordinary civilian clothes. Sometimes incredibly foul-mouthed, sometimes drunk. Beautiful speaking voice—and courage! One ship that he was on, I will never forget it as long as I live. She had been loaded up too deep with benzine[20] and, coming back through the Red Sea[21] in a

---

16 [Presumably this is where the Eldon failed to understand a word, or it may have been censored. However, there is Penrhyn in Barry and a Penryn in Falmouth.]
17 [The Spanish Civil War of 1936–9. The Nationalists, who were attempting to overthrow the Republic, were supported by the fascists in Italy and Nazi Germany.]
18 [A port in south-eastern Spain.]
19 [Another Spanish port; about 150 km south of Valencia.]
20 [A light, highly flammable petroleum ether probably to be added to fuel. Different to the chemical compound of benzene (C_6H_6).]
21 [So heading towards the Suez Canal and the Mediterranean Sea after loading in the Middle East.]

temperature of 115,[22] she caught some sort of a fire and the skipper ordered "Abandon Ship!"

If you could only imagine the Red Sea, that beautiful bright blue sea, perfectly calm, perfectly still, blazing blue sky, and the ship just standing there. At any moment she is going to blow up, and Nick Tamlin is there in the boat with the mate, and one hundred yards away the skipper in a boat with the rest of the crew, and they lay on their oars watching, and the ship still stands there, and the skipper said: "Shall we go back on board boys, and see what we can do? Any volunteers?"

There may be one in a couple of thousand who would have had the courage to go back on her. I know I wouldn't. Nick Tamlin says: "Yes, I'm going", and he went back on board and helped to put the fire out, and they brought their ship back; and Nick Tamlin received the Lloyd's Cross, our highest decoration of award.[23]

Whenever I think of that man, of his courage and his integrity and his bravery and the way he would always sneer at those who were not with him, I am always reminded of a thing I read once in a book about a King of England who was fighting in France. They had fought all day and they knew that the next morning all sorts of troops were coming up against them, and one of his men turned round and said, "I wish we could have some men from England here to help us fight", and the King said these words: "If we are to die, we are enough to do our country loss: if to live, the fewer men the greater share of honour. If there is any man here who hath no stomach for this fight, let him speak forth. His passport shall be made and crowns for convoy put into his purse."[24]

---

22 [115°F; this is 46°C.]
23 [Lloyd's of London, the marine insurance market, have four medals: Lloyd's Medal for Saving Life at Sea, Lloyd's Medal for Meritorious Service, Lloyd's Medal for Services to Lloyd's and Lloyd's War Medal for Bravery at Sea.]
24 [An edited version of what is known as the "St Crispin's Day Speech" by King Henry from Shakespeare's *Henry V.*]

MY NAME IS FRANK

I know you will curse me for saying this, but the fact remains—you know it as well as I do—we've been going to sea all our lives, it's the only job we know, it's the only job we want. We shall keep sailing out.

But before I have finished this talk, I just want to tell you the nicest little yarn that I have come across alongshore sides yet. It is about a sailor who had just come back after a seven months' trip. He's been dive-bombed, he's been shelled, he's been raided, he's been mined; he's done everything, and he's walking down the street with a deep-sea roll and his best civvies on, and an old lady comes along to him and pins a white feather on to him,[25] and he picks the feather out and says, "Lady, why can't you bend a duck round this?"

Good-bye boys.

---

25 [The Order of the White Feather was an organisation formed during the First World War. Women would present white feathers to men who were not in uniform in order to shame them into enlisting. The campaign was resurrected during Second World War. There are many anecdotes of brave men having been given white feathers in error.]

5. British Corporal

YOU HAVE HEARD IN my last broadcast[26] about a dive-bombing attack. Well, really a dive-bombing attack is nothing very new because, to be quite candid, I was on a ship in 1937 or 1938—I'm not quite sure which it was—and we had a dive-bombing attack, practically the first of this series of this war on a ship.

I was on the *British Corporal*,[27] a British tanker, and we were pushing through the Mediterranean. We had loaded up at Abadan and were coming through to discharge at Avonmouth. And at that time the Spanish war was in full flight, and the *Luftwaffe* was absolutely on the top line. They had no anti-aircraft defence to consider. They had no balloons. They had nothing at all. They could merely come sweeping down on their nice little low-level bombing attacks and lay their eggs where and as they pleased. Hence, the fact that they won in Spain.

I'll never forget that attack. It was in the morning about six o'clock, I was stand-by the quartermaster, standing on the wing of the bridge looking idly round, and I watched the second cook rub the sleep out of his eyes as he trudged along the for'ard well-deck along to the forepeak complete with the galley boy. They got hold of a rope, threw it down the forepeak and they lashed a barrel of flour on it; and I could see the poor old second and the galley boy heaving and straining and tugging, and finally they got the barrel of flour up on the deck. Put the hatch boards back, unbent the rope, and away they started trundling it along the deck.

Very, very nice scene!—sea was as calm as glass, no wind, just nice calm, cool, early morning in the Mediterranean and I heard an aeroplane.

---

26 This is talk nine.
27 [See page 61.]

Well, at that time an aeroplane was—you might call it a novelty. We called it a novelty at sea, and I watched the little speck approaching and he came along closer and closer and closer. And then suddenly he swooped right down on our starboard beam, flashing right past us; and I heard a funny sort of rattling noise and I thought at first it was coal in the bunkers sliding about and then I realised he was firing a machine-gun at us.

I made one duck down underneath, dashed up on to the bridge, and the skipper was looking absolutely petrified with astonishment. The second cook was trundling the barrel along the well-deck. Round came the plane back again in one swooping dive right on top of us. And then the crash—I'd never heard anything like it—as a bomb dropped in the water about fifty yards on the starboard beam. And we were loaded with benzine.

The skipper—we've always called him a cantankerous old bloke—but immediately he was alert on the *qui vive*,[28] and he gave orders for zigzagging. Hard to starboard went the quartermaster, and she started away practically at right angles to her course. All hands came up and a greaser on watch below, the four-to-eight greaser, poked a weary greasy face from out of the fiddly (stokehold) and said, "What's all this?" and went down below again. And the second cook continued to trundle his barrel.

Back came the plane right down over the foremast and machine-gunned us. The skipper remained there on the bridge like an iron man, zigzagging hard to port.

That plane dive-bombed us, that plane, the pride of the *Luftwaffe*, came down on top of us, and we hadn't even a balloon on the end of the stick to defend ourselves with. She screamed down on top of us and laid her eggs all over the ocean, and we had 15,000 tons of benzine on board and they couldn't hit us.

---

28 [Latin for "who lives" but it is meant as being on lookout in this sense.]

And back he came, foremast high, right across the ship, port and starboard, splattering his eggs all over the ocean. Raining machine-gun bullets all round us, and he never hit us. He must have altered the bed of the Mediterranean quite considerably. And then he circled round us again and again. And the skipper was still on the bridge, and the second cook and the cabin boy were under the flying bridge.

I remember I met the second cook in Cardiff afterwards and he said, "Do you know what that there dratted boy said to me as we were there under the bridge?" I said, "No, why, what did he say?"

"Well", he said, "that Jerry came down and was covering the deck with machine-gun bullets, and you know what the tank tops were like at the time?"—I said "Yes."

"Well", he said, "the boy gets hold of me by the arm and says, 'Don't they make lovely red sparks when they hit the deck?'"

6. Talk to Seamen, Liverpool

HULLO SHIPMATES, HOW ARE you keeping? I'm a sailor also, but so far I'm ashore recuperating from one or two things that happened to me at sea. But I would like to know how you are getting on. In any case, I wonder how you're listening to this. Maybe the quartermaster's at the wheel and the skipper has his wireless going full blast. Maybe you're the bo'sun or the carpenter, old chippy sitting there in his cabin wondering what he's got to do for the next day and wondering what jobs he's got to do, with all the boys hanging round the door just listening to this programme.

Well, this is a real sailor speaking to you. I shall speak in our own slang, in case anyone should possibly want to interfere. And I shall tell you that I am a Bluey Boy.[29] You know what a Bluey Boy is out in Liverpool, but I know how dreadfully worried you all get when you're out at sea, wondering about what's happening at home.

Well, if you're anybody listening to me from Liverpool, well let me tell you this, that we're doing fine. The old port at Liverpool is keeping flat wide open. They're coming in and they're going out and they're being turned round. Everything's a little quiet round here, but not too bad. We're having a pretty good time, as a matter of fact, but you out at sea—Gosh! I wish I was with you.

I hope that there's someone on British tankers who's listening to me now, and you're pushing up past the Twelve Apostles.[30] I wonder if it will be the second dog-watch and

---

29 Bluey Boys = blue water sailor, a deep sea man. [That is a sailor of the world's oceans, not coastal sailing.]
30 [A collection of islands or high mountains in the Red Sea. Finding an exact location has not been possible.]

Frank Laskier

all the boys are sort of gathering round; and you've done your dhobying, and you've given the Peggy[31] a piece of your mind, and you've cursed the cook up hill and down dale, and you're sitting there talking as you always talk and as you always will talk—SHIP. Day in and day out. Never anything else. Ships you've been on, ships you wanted to go on, ships that you've cursed, bad ones and healthy ones, beautiful ones.

Remember that lovely trip you did last trip?—Your last trip was always the best wasn't it? But you keep your spirits up; just keep sailing and keep sailing. There's all sorts of boys here, and if you had to listen to a lot of people talking, you'd get the idea that we come ashore and we stay ashore for months and months and months, and finally the police come and get hold of us and drag us off to ships.

War or no war, they're still going crazy at the Board of Trade, they can't get enough men for the ships. Because there just aren't enough sailors in Liverpool to cope with our shipping. They're pushing off out—Gosh! There's four fellows live next door to me. They've come back, one fellow from a nine months' trip—and he's not crazy, either. He's had ten days ashore, and he's pushing off out again the same as was always done.

And remember this, boys. When this war is over and when peace has settled down and the skipper's hanging his dhobying on the Hotchkiss[32] mounting on the bridge, and you can go and take your stroll along the poop and not see the old 4-inch gun[33]—when the war is over we'll know and we'll talk about the things we did. We'll remember all those brave fellows who we knew; the funny times that we've had, times

---

31 Peggy = boy.
32 [This is probably the French-made machine gun of ·303 calibre that was intended to be used as a defence against attacks by aircraft.]
33 [This is perhaps a breech-loading gun first made in 1908. These guns were reused as coastal artillery and for arming merchant ships during the Second World War.]

that we've come back out of convoy with a load of meat or a load of fruit and said "To blazes with 'em", and we've got through. We've got past a submarine, we've got past the dive bombers, we've got through the mine-fields and we've come home. And we've sailed out. We always *will* sail out.

7. Forty-three Days in an Open Boat

I HAD HAD A PRETTY bad packet at sea, and I was put on to a naval hospital ship, and had rather a bad time, and finally I was getting better—recuperating. And one afternoon I shall never forget—I heard a bumping sort of scrape along the ship's side—we were anchored out in midstream—and we sort of knew, with that electrical tension that goes through a sickbay ward, that there were some new patients coming on board, and I eased myself up out of bed, sat on my pillows, and watched.

The door opened at the end of the ward, and in came the stewards carrying stretchers, and they passed along just close to me, and I could see those stretchers, with blankets over them, and underneath the funny, queer, shrivelled little … skeleton—of a man. And I watched them as the stewards walked slowly through the ward as they carried them into the medical ward. And I lay back in bed and wondered what on earth had happened to those men—and then I found out later—I was talking to one of the stewards.

It appears that three men, these three men, had been torpedoed on Christmas Eve. Their ship had been proceeding nicely and steadily. And suddenly there was a explosion, and the ship stopped dead under the impact and started to sink. These men—four of them—crawled into a boat, and they pushed away and watched their ship sinking—on Christmas Eve. And they were thirty days in the boat—and they were thirty-three days in the boat—and they were thirty-seven days in the boat—without shelter, without comfort, without security and with Death, like an armed man, standing by them.

And the thirty-seventh day their food gave out. They had no more food—not even a tiny little morsel, that little crust no bigger than your thumbnail of hard, ship's biscuit. Even that was gone. They had licked their condensed milk tins dry; they had scoured out the bottoms of their little bully-beef tins; they had no more food. And three days after that, their water gave out, and they spent seven days without water, relying on the dew that fell, on the tiny little tropical rainstorms that came down.

And they were finally picked up; one of them had died, and the other three were living skeletons, so weak that they couldn't give their names, so weak that they couldn't think, so weak that they were dying.

And these three, little shrivelled husks of men were brought on board the naval hospital ship and they lay there on water-beds—mattresses filled with water at a little less than blood heat—and they started to get better. And in three weeks' time those men, members of the Merchant Service, were fit to go home. I wasn't quite fit, but when I did get home, I went along to the house of one—his name was—well, we'll just call him Bill. I knew his address and I went along—he'd told me about his wife, and everything—and I went along to meet Bill again and to see how he was getting on and to take him out for a pint of bitter at the local.

And I went to the door, and his wife came, and I said "Where's Bill?" and she said, "Oh, Bill?—Bill?—oh, Bill was home for about ten days and he couldn't stick it. He signed on about a fortnight ago.

(Recording ended here abruptly.)

8. Tough Mate

IN THE MERCHANT SERVICE we call our chief officers mates; and when I came back from my hospital ship, where I had been getting better from my own wounds, we had several people on board who had also been shipwrecked, and amongst them there was the mate of a ship that sailed from Liverpool.

He was a little man, the size of two-penny-worth of copper,[34] about 5 feet 4 inches, very, very sunburned, and with that far-away glint in his eye which you always get in a deep-sea man. I often used to wonder why, what he was doing, what his story was, and how he happened to be coming back; and he never told me, he never told anybody. But I finally got the story from one member of the crew of the lifeboat in which McCarthy had spent such a long time—his name was McCarthy. His ship had been torpedoed about 800 miles from land, and McCarthy and twelve other men got into a lifeboat and they watched their ship sink. They were in the tropics, pretty rough sea, and they spent the first twenty-four hours and they never touched their food or their water, and then, when they opened up their water canisters after twenty-four hours, the water was brackish, there was salt in it.

They spent seven days on that boat, seven days, and seven nights, with a tiny morsel of biscuit to eat, if they could eat it, and no water. And thirst was upon them, death was standing by them, and these men sailed that boat and rowed that boat, with never a murmur, and McCarthy sat there at the tiller and kept her on her course and kept their spirits up,

---

34 [Copper here refers to low-value coins, which were minted using a copper-based metal. At the time there would have been a farthing (a quarter of a penny), a halfpenny and a penny.]

MY NAME IS FRANK

and there was never a murmur for seven days and seven nights—without a drop of water.

And on the morning of the eighth day they came across an enemy tramp steamer.[35] They pulled their boat alongside, and McCarthy climbed up the blistered side of this tramp, up the Jacob's ladder,[36] on to the deck and up on to the bridge, and there, to use our own expression, he lowered the boom[37] on the ship's company for food and for water and for cigarettes and for tobacco, and for maps and things like that.

All was lowered into the boat, and the boat laid off, and the captain turned round to McCarthy and said: "You can't go back in that boat, you are a belligerent.[38] You have a Marine in the boat, I can see his cap." And McCarthy, with seven days' starvation, seven days of thirst, seven days of frantic worry, and seven hundred years of sea tradition behind him, turned round on the skipper and laid him out cold—and took a flying jump over the side, a 40-foot dive into shark-infested waters, and swam to his own boat and made sail and got the oars out and beat them to it and dodged them in the dark, and brought that lifeboat 700 miles back, into Bathurst.[39]

When I met him he was coming home in a suit three sizes too big for him, that had once belonged to the Governor of Bathurst. McCarthy, tough mate, never said a word, not a syllable. He had merely done his job.

---

35 [Such a vessel does not have a fixed schedule and is available to charter on the open market for transporting freight. It originates from the same word meaning an itinerant person.]
36 [A rope ladder with wooden rungs.]
37 [Most sources explain that to "lower the boom" is to reprimand or treat someone harshly. Perhaps, here, Frank's meaning was that the crew were nagged into handing over items.]
38 [Someone who is engaged in fighting a war.]
39 [There is a Bathurst Harbour in Tasmania, Australia.]

9. The Dive Bomber

SAILING AT SEA THESE days is by no means the job it was in the last war. In the last war you merely had your surface raider to look after or your periscope to look out for, or your occasional minefield. But in this one, you've got a combination of all those together, and added to that you have something that you can only describe in the biblical words: "The terror that flies by night."[40] Only it's not night, it's the dive bombers.

We've just about got him taped now, believe me, because when we get in the danger area we *know* that all sorts of things can happen to us. But principally we can expect a submarine, and we get the old 4-inch gun ready and we have her loaded; and we are standing down, and we get the Hotchkiss gun out, and we clean it and polish it and we practise with it and we are all set and ready.

And the ship goes on doing her steady 200 miles a day, and you get closer and closer and closer into that area, and the sea turns from black into deep green, and you know that you are coming in, and you're coming in, but you're waiting for him. You've got a *gun*—you can *defend* yourself!

And one evening, out of a clear sky, he'll come on you. You see him there, right up in the distance, a tiny little speck, and you whip out your binoculars and you look at him and you say, "Now, what is it, what is it—is it a Lockheed,[41] is it a Sunderland?"[42] And you watch it, and suddenly an idea flashes across the back of your mind: "My God! it is!" and you make one flying dive towards the Hotchkiss, and you scream out "Aircraft attack!"

---

40 [Psalm 91:5: "Thou shalt not be afraid for the terror by night; nor for the arrow that flieth by day".]
41 [Probably the US made P-38 Lightning, a fighter-bomber.]
42 [The Sunderland was a flying boat bomber made by Short Brothers in Belfast.]

Whip the covers off; she's loaded and ready. Get behind, he's coming down to you, he's coming down, and the noise is screaming and screaming, and you think to yourself, "My God! He's coming for me, for *me!* for *ME!*" And you're standing there, and you can feel the sweat running down the backs of your knees. Then he gets closer and closer, and you can see those horrible splashes of the bullets as they come across the water and go ripping across the deck—and there's a noise like the opening of the gates of hell, and he's gone—and he's dropped his bombs—and he's missed you!

And you stick another clip in, and you wait for him to come back—and he will come back, and he gets his sights all set, and he has you there, dead ready, and he comes down in a screaming, tearing dive, and you stand there and you're *paralysed* with fright and you don't know which way your deflection is and you don't know whether your gun will be properly loaded and you don't know whether you oughtn't to drop the whole damn thing and go over the side—and you pray—and he comes close to you—and you let one little burst go out, and you see the tracer bullets, and you say "God! I've GOT him!"

"Switch it just a little over to starboard—Let her go, boys, he's going right into it!" And he does—he walks right into the bullets—right smack into them! He gives one enormous leap into the air, like a tremendous hiccup—UP—and then *down*—and he crashes—and you leave your gun, and you go and look over the side, and you watch it there in the water—a funny little black blob.

Then the skipper turns round and says: "Well, boys, they don't deserve it, they wouldn't do it to us—they're only rats! But go on—lower the boat—pick 'em up!" And we pick 'em up.

If there are any Nazi airmen listening to this, I wish them joy of their job. Personally, I'd much rather have a good Hotchkiss.

10. City of Benares, San Demetrio, Eurylochus

I AM A SAILOR, AN Englishman, and my first name is Frank. I am quite an ordinary sort of individual—all we sailors are. We have our job to do and we do it. You can see me or my mates anywhere in the whole world; you can find us in Joey's Saloon in Montreal, or you can find us dancing in the Trocadero in Brisbane, or you can find us getting slightly kettled in Jack Dempsey's Bar in New York. We don't wear any uniform. We have a small silver badge.[43]

Well, when this war first started the Navy sent round asking us what we would like to do—whether we would want to have Navy personnel on board our ships to man the guns; or whether we would like to train and handle them ourselves. Well, naturally, we said we would defend our own ships. And so we all went to schools started all over in the seaports of England, and we learnt how to handle the 4-inch gun and the anti-aircraft gun, and everything going.

We started this war—we entered into this war—we, the sailors, with a distinct understanding in our own souls that we would fight clean. Well, all sorts of things happened to us; some of us did long and unpleasant trips in prison ships, others were torpedoed and spent—one man I know spent as much as forty-three days in an open boat. But we didn't mind; we were young and we were strong and we were healthy. And then things started to happen to us.

I found a ship in Liverpool and I found out, as we will on board ship before we sail, that she was taking evacuee

---

43 [A small silver metal badge featuring the letters MN beneath a naval crown.]

children to Canada.[44] I was so scared at the thought of taking those children, and I was so scared of anybody getting to know about it, that I even gave my allotment note[45] to the Post Office with the instructions that they would send it to my mother five days after I had sailed. So that even my poor old mother wouldn't even know the name of the ship that I was on.

Well, we sailed out from Liverpool; we scouted round the coast of England, and one night we picked the children up and we went out. It was the happiest and yet the most dreadful trip I had ever done in my life. Of course those children, they were *ordinary* children, boys and girls in between nine and twelve; little boys and little girls so pathetically seasick at first, and so wonderfully bright afterwards. They used to come up on the gun and look on us with awe, astonishment and fear, and ask us to open the breach so that they could look up the muzzle. And generally we had a beautiful time.

We wore our eyelids out, looking for submarines; we did watch and watch and watch and watch, and finally we got them safely into Montreal. We sailed up the St. Lawrence and we handed them over to the kind care of friends who were waiting for them; and we rubbed our hands together and we said: "Boys, that was a good trip, that's over", and we went into Joey's, and we bought ourselves a few beers. We loaded up with food and we came back to England. We had no children on board for the return journey.

Five days out from England I was on watch on the poop, and I saw six *query*.[46] We trained the gun on it, because the

---

44 [As many British cities were at risk from aerial bombardment, the government arranged for children to be moved to safer places in the UK or within the British Empire, in this case Canada.]
45 [This was a scheme under the Merchant Shipping Acts where a seaman could arrange for part of his wages to be paid to a relative.]
46 [Perhaps "six lifebelts and a boat".]

Frank Laskier

Hun[47] has a very nice habit of hiding a submarine behind a boat. We saw no one in the boat—no sign of life. We sailed right up to it. We made a lee,[48] and I was one of the men who went down over the side, and we put grapples on the lifeboat and we hauled it up over the side and swung her inboard.

In that boat, laying in the bottom, there were sixteen dead children; ordinary children, may be the little boy or girl who lived next door to you. Children! And their faces were blue and pinched with the cold, and their little hands and knees were covered with scratches and blood where they had gone down the ship's side into that boat. Some of them had little nightdresses on; others were half-dressed, others were fully dressed. Their lifebelts had cut rings and grooves and chafed with saltwater round their necks; and we stood—the men of that ship, looking at that lifeboat, and we swore by everything we held holy that we would be avenged.

Because we know—we sailors know since—they had waited for the *City of Benares*.[49] I am sorry if anybody listening to me had children on the *City of Benares*—it's opening up old wounds I know, but it's infinitely better that these old wounds should be opened and remain open to the end of the war than we who are left, strong and healthy, should forget about it. Sixteen dead children! On a cold winter's evening, 500 miles from land. Dead! I can't forget it. Will you ever forget it?

---

47 [A nickname for Germans. It appears to have originated from Kaiser Wilhelm's speech to troops departing to fight in the Boxer rebellion of 1900. The Huns were a nomadic people from central Asia and Wilhelm used this as a theme in his completely over-the-top rhetoric: "Just as a thousand years ago the Huns under their King Attila made a name for themselves, one that even today makes them seem mighty in history and legend, may the name German be affirmed by you in such a way in China that no Chinese will ever again dare to look cross-eyed at a German." It was called *Hunnenrede* (the Hun speech) and Allied propagandists picked up on "Hun" during the First World War as an abusive term for Germans.]
48 [Leeward is downwind.]
49 [See page 62 for a description of this ship.]

We came back from the *City of Benares*. We buried our cargo at sea; we separated and we went on other boats, and stranger and even more horrible things happened to us.

Then we did another trip. I came back, and one evening in a pub I was talking to an old shipmate of mine, and he told me of something that had happened. He was on a boat; he had said good-bye to his wife knowing that he was going out on a benzine tanker—and, believe me, even in peace time a benzine tanker is no picnic. They went over to America and loaded her up with benzine and they brought her back. Those men sat on top of 15,000 tons of benzine—15,000 tons of benzine that had to be taken straight out of the ship and put straight into a bomber.

Coming back their convoy was attacked; a German raider appeared on the horizon, and with their superior guns and their superior range, she shelled the convoy. Five shots landed on board the ship and the midship house, and burst it into flames, ripped it wide open. Another shot landed on the after well-deck and burst the tank tops open. The ship was ablaze—she was flooded with benzine—and the captain ordered "Abandon ship". They went over the side and into one boat filled with about fourteen survivors under the charge of the second mate, a man named Hawkins.

Well, as they got into the boat, Hawkins was looking out and he saw the last man coming down the ladder. He was a greaser and his name was Boyle or Doyle, I am not sure which, and as he came down the gangway he slipped and he fell across the gunwale of the boat, and he picked himself up and his face was the colour of a bucketful of ashes.

They pushed the boat off and left their blazing ship, and went out into the waters of the Atlantic—mid-Atlantic—the Atlantic in a gale; and for two days those men were adrift on the Western Ocean in that boat. They were safe, as safe as I am sitting here, as safe as you are in your homes, because that was the *Jervis Bay*[50] convoy, and they knew that they were going to be picked up—that destroyers were out looking for them. And during that time Harry Boyle had stayed in the boat; he'd never shirked his watch, he'd bailed, he'd steered, he'd kept a lookout, and he had never complained.

After two days they came across the *San Demetrio*.[51] She was still ablaze but she was still floating, and those men—those fourteen men—went back on board and they put the fire out; and they sealed the decks up, and with the aid of a lifeboat compass and a Philips' Atlas,[52] without stores, without radio, and without help, they brought that ship back into England with 12,000 tons of benzine on board her. And Paddy Boyle was an engine-room man, and he crawled up the ladder on board the *Demetrio* and he went down into the engine-room and he watched for two days and for two nights without rest or respite, or sleep, and he never complained.

And in the evening of the second day, Paddy went up aloft to his room, and laid down on his bunk, and died. And when they went to pick him up he just hadn't any ribs; when he'd fallen across the gunwale of the boat he'd stove them in.

They buried him at sea, under the Union Jack—a sailor's grave, a sailor's death.

But they brought 12,000 tons of aviation spirit home for England, and that same spirit was intended to go into a bomber that would scream over Berlin and scream over Hamburg and blast the daylight out of them and leave them in the misery and desolation that they have caused all over the world. That benzine will go into tanks that will go down the Unter den Linden;[53] and those men who have been chased out of Dunkirk and tricked and cheated will be behind those guns

---

50 [See page 65.]
51 [See page 62.]
52 [Probably refers to *Philips' Mercantile Marine Atlas of the World* published by George Philip & Son.]
53 [A large boulevard that runs from east to west in central Berlin. It means under the linden (lime trees).]

on the day of victory, on the day of the sailors' vengeance. But they didn't bring that benzine back to put in joy-riding cars.

That point is one that's a sore point with me. If you people will only realise that no matter what you are doing, the food you eat, that the petrol you use, that the clothes you wear, that the cigarettes you smoke and matches that you strike to light the cigarettes, that the plush on the cinema seats—that everything—everything in England, is brought over by the sailors. We will never let you down; we will go through trials unimaginable; we'll fight and we'll fight and we'll sail, and we'll bring back your food.

If I were merely sitting here giving this—can we call it talk?—merely to ask you for money, how easy it would be. You'd merely dig into your pockets or your cheque-books, and you'd give me all the money I wanted. But we don't want money. There's a scheme on foot these days; all over the world you see the letter "V". All over occupied Europe, all over England, is that "V". We have brought you your food. But for us the "V" stands for victory, and for *vengeance*.

A long time ago I had four friends, four shipmates, four schoolmates. In 1938 we came back and we decided that as we were all great friends we would have a holiday ashore. We had a marvellous time; we were happy and we were sunburned, and Charlie had his wife. And I always look back on that as a sort of calm before the storm, of this storm. You see, to digress for one moment, Charlie and I were very great friends and we both fell in love with the same girl. Well, she was a very, very wise girl; she chose the infinitely better man—she chose Charlie. Okay! I came to their wedding, I was Charlie's best man; we had a marvellous time and they were both happy.

Out of those four men I sit here now with a funny little grotesque stump where a perfectly good right foot used to be. Billie was blown to hell on a minesweeper; George went down with the *Courageous*.[54] Let me tell you what happened to Charlie.

Charlie was on my ship with me, and we signed on, and he was very, very unhappy when we had to push off. We went out in convoy and we faced the dive-bombers and we faced the submarines, and twenty-one days out the convoy sort of broke up and we went our various ways.

We settled down to the ordinary routine life of a ship at sea, and one night—800 miles from land—I was on watch on the gun. At half-past six it was pitch dark on a tropical night. Suddenly there was a shot and a bang, and into the air there shot an enormous great yellow flare. I turned round and made one wild dash for the gun, and as I got to the gun, suddenly a hell, an absolute holocaust of shells burst around us. They were firing on the starboard beam, complete broadsides, those six 11-inch guns and eight 5.9-inch guns.

Quick, up to the gun, open the breech, ram the shell, ram the charge home, close the oven door, stick the tube in, run to the trainer, train her round, quick, quick, and crash the shells are banging into us.

Round she's trained, the lights are there, try to get on the searchlight, duck under the muzzle, put your range on, bring it down, bring it down; pull the trigger. Bang went old Mildred! It was heaven.

Back aft, open up again, put the shell in, and then ... there was a crash like the opening of the Gates of Hell!

I was thrown about six feet. I picked myself up and there was just no gun worth speaking of left. Up to my feet, round the poop, down the ladder, across the well-deck, stepping on a bloody gruel of men's bodies who had been smashed as they came out of the poop; up the ladder, along the upper deck. God, where's the bridge?—There isn't any. The captain is shouting: "Abandon ship". The great glaring eye of a

---

54 [See page 65.]

searchlight is blazing down on us. I turn to go aft and there on the deck is Charlie.

I never thought that any man could be so horribly wounded, and still live.

If you are listening, Mary, I have to apologise to you. I told you that Charlie died quickly and quietly, with a bullet through his head; but it doesn't matter, Mary, there are a lot of people listening to this, in the fo'c'sles of ships, and they will remember; remember that "V"; remember the vengeance. Remember; remember what we have been through; remember what we're going through; and fight, and fight, and never, never, never give in!

(The name of Frank's ship was *Eurylochus*.[55])
(The raider that sank her was the *Admiral Scheer*.[56])

---

55 [See page 64.]
56 [See page 66. Records indicate *Eurylochus* was in fact sunk by the *Kormoran*. It is not clear as to the reason for this discrepancy. It could be confusion as a result of the chaos of war or perhaps the circumstances were altered for propaganda purposes.]

11. On a Raft

WHEN YOU THINK OF a raft, you nearly always think of the illustration in *Robinson Crusoe*,[57] of Robinson on the raft. You know, a collection of boards tied together, with the mast and with the sail, a shirt and a couple of packing cases on it. But that isn't a raft.

The raft that we had been on when our ship had been sunk was the size of about six orange boxes, lashed together. Full oil drums, empty oil drums, and the sea was like green glass, with beautiful lights of phosphorus underneath. And we went over the side and swam, and there were sharks, and we *knew* there were sharks.

In a crazy hysteria of fear, we crawled on to the rafts.

I remember them so well as they came on. There was Mac wounded, MacDavid the second engineer. You know the old story by Kipling,[58] that you've only got to go down into the engine-room of any ship east of Suez and shout "Mac" and someone is bound to come up. He was there. The junior "sparks" was there. The two little midshipmen were there. I was there. The extra fourth mate and the skipper, and the chief engineer.

Well, we huddled there together on that raft, and there were shouts and shouts, "Let go the painter"[59]—She was tied to the boat, she was *tied,* and the boat was going down. We could see her going down. And suddenly, someone found a knife, and slashed and hacked away at the painter, and the raft floated free.

---

57 [The book by Daniel Defoe published in 1719. Some people consider this to be the first English novel.]
58 [Rudyard Kipling wrote many, many stories and this recollection could be from *Captains Courageous, Mandalay* (the source of "East of Eden"), or *McAndrew's Hymn.*]
59 [A rope used to secure a small boat.]

And we lay there on the raft, wounded—horribly wounded. And suddenly, without any cause or reason whatsoever, the raft overturned.

Just imagine to sit and feel the raft slipping and slipping from underneath you, and the water getting closer round you.

And then, suddenly, the raft had overturned.

But we got back, the skipper got back, and the chief engineer, and we grabbed hold of poor old Mac by the scruff of his neck, and dragged him on board, and they dragged me on board. And from somewhere, or somehow, they picked up an extra Chinese, and they dragged him on board.

And we watched our ship sinking.

I was very, very fortunate. I was on the raft and I had been, let us say, so seriously wounded, that I was losing consciousness. But I remember two or three things that happened to me, and I don't think I'll ever forget them.

The warmth and the security, and the infinite love and tenderness, which one man—I'll never know who it was—kept his arm about me the whole time, to prevent me from slipping off.

I remember MacDavid, the second engineer, as he sat on the far end of the raft, with that little oar about three-foot long, smacking away to scare the sharks.

I remember the sharks, blue, green and grey, as they swept up from the depths of the ocean to make huge vicious snaps at my legs. I remember the rasping, grasping sound, as they scraped along the bottom of the raft. But they didn't get us.

And all that night, and all that day, and all the next night.

I wonder if you can understand what I mean when I say that. All that night, twelve hours, and that day, twelve hours. But throughout the whole of that time, the wounded did not complain, and the healthy helped.

Throughout the whole of that time, the skipper was never referred to as anything else other than "Sir". There were no complaints. There were no faintings. We stuck it. Holding on, for we knew, we knew that the raft was sinking. Those little oil drums had been pierced.

And then the smoke on the horizon. And the little midshipman, our first-trip midshipman, stood up on that raft and balanced himself on ten by eight of drifting planks, and put his coat through an oar and waved it, and saved our lives.

And I lay there on the raft as the Spanish tramp steamer came alongside, and they'd lowered an enormous great fish-basket to put us in. And I saw the basket coming closer and closer and I lifted myself up and balanced on one leg and made a wild grab at this basket, as someone suddenly seized me by the seat of the trousers, and lifted me inside. But just as I left the raft, a horrible, burning, stinging pain went through my left foot, my remaining left foot, and it wasn't until later that I found out what it was. The sea had made a last bite at me. I'd been stung by a jelly-fish.

12. Meeting the Navy

THERE HAS ALWAYS, IN some indefinable way, been an antagonism between members of the Navy and the Merchant Service, because we are both doing the same job, and both do it in an entirely different way.

Let me tell you how I last met the Royal Navy.

I was on a Spanish tramp steamer, and very, very sick indeed. I had been three and a half days without any medical attention whatsoever, but that is beside the point.

I was sick, and as I lay in my bunk, in the little hospital of this tramp, a man came in and said to me, "There's an armed merchant cruiser on the horizon". And I remember I sort of passed out after he said that because, as I came to, instead of finding my little cabin so calm and so bare, it was full of men, full of sailors, and I remember that I felt as though a man were putting binoculars in front of my eyes. One moment everything would be large, and the next moment they would recede to little tiny pin points.

I was getting delirious, I suppose, and as I lay there utterly helpless gazing at them, suddenly they seemed to part, and a man pushed his way to the front, and he wore the red and gold epaulettes of a surgeon of the Royal Navy. And he leaned forward, and I'll never forget him. He had even found out my first name. Because he got hold of me so gently by the arm, and shook me, and said, "Don't worry, Frank, we're here, we'll look after you. Now don't worry, we're going to put you to sleep now."

And they pricked my arm with squirts and they put morphia into me. Oh! it was heavenly. All the grinding searing pain had gone. I felt I was floating away on the top of a cloud, and they lifted me and whisked me outside. They cut away my clothes, they wrapped me in a blanket, and carried me in a flexible stretcher, and laid me down on the deck just by the gangway, ready to lower me into the boat. And as I laid there, on the deck of that steamer, under God's blue sky, and I looked and saw my skipper with the light of hope shining in his eyes, and Mac laying there beside me, safe, and all the rest of we boys who had been on that raft. And I saw in front of me the huge mass of that armed merchant cruiser and, standing by me, two men in the spotless white of the Royal Navy.

Suddenly, something peculiar happened to me, something I've never experienced before in all my life. I had a funny sort of constricting pain in my chest, and a burning sensation in my throat and my eyes. It had never happened before, and I didn't know what it was. But I found that I was crying. I missed my friends, I missed the men who had helped me.

I lay there on the deck of that ship, and cried not only from grief, but from happiness and from safety.

13. Sea Raider

(This was the *Admiral Scheer*.[60] Frank, when he made the recording, by the way, had never heard a Quentin Reynolds broadcast.[61])

To add to this series, I've told you exactly what happened to me on board the ship. Perhaps without intending to, because at one time, the memory was so fresh in my mind, that I did not feel inclined to talk about it, or think about it, but now you know, I am the sailor called Frank. One of thousands.

I could tell you my name, but it doesn't matter. It is of no importance. My name might be "Smith" or "Jones" or "Brown" or "Robinson" or anything. I am merely a sailor.

And I have been through things, and I have seen them.

I could give all sorts of messages to you, if I were merely sitting here asking you for money, it would be so dreadfully easy. I know that you would give me anything that I wanted.

But, there is another thing. This is a world-wide broadcast, and there is one man listening to me to-night, and I have a word for him.

I wonder if you remember me, Mister. I wonder.

You're the captain of a German raider, and on the 29th January you attacked a merchant ship. Don't you remember? Just when it was dark, you saw me then. You met me. At one time you weren't more than 100 yards from me. You followed us up. You chased us. You kept hidden. You were afraid even of our 4-inch gun, against your 11-inch guns.

You attacked us in the dark, at point-blank range. Don't you remember? Don't you remember shelling us for twenty

---

60 [Records indicate that the *Eurylochus* was sunk by the *Kormoran* not the *Admiral Scheer*. See note 56, page 46.]
61 [Reynolds was an American war correspondent who reported from Britain. He narrated, for example, *London Can Take It!*, a short propaganda film from 1940 intended to instill support from Americans.]

minutes and then ceasing fire, and coming round to examine the damage.

I was on the starboard bunker hatch, you shone your searchlight on me. You'd shot my foot off. Don't you remember the fourth mate making a signal out to you that we were abandoning ship? And you answered the signal. Don't you remember opening fire on us again?

I remember it. We got on to the raft, didn't we? You saw us, you watched our ship sink. And you machine-gunned us. But you didn't do the job properly. Because out of that ship's company ten men are alive, and those ten men know what you did.

Three of us were wounded. Seven of us were not. Those seven are back at sea.

You'd be surprised if you knew the job that the captain has. You'd be surprised, and I don't think you'd be very happy about it, either.

You murdered my shipmates. You stood by and watched us drown. You machine-gunned us.

But go ahead, Mister. Go right ahead.

Using your yellow, filthy, murderous methods, you may get another couple more ships. You work the same stunt on them. You'll leave them to the sharks, won't you?

But, your time is up.

Sooner or later, and it will be sooner, you will be met by the Navy.

Aircraft from the Fleet Air Arm will come over you, and they'll bomb you and blast you and your bridge will fly to pieces, as ours did, and your decks will burst open as ours did.[62]

And then a battleship will come alongside, and I hope it's the *Warspite*.[63] And with her 15-inch guns she'll fire you, and

---

62 [Frank's hope came true and the *Admiral Scheer* was sunk by RAF bombs.]
63 [See page 67.]

you will see your crew dead and dying. You will see your ship blowing up, and you yourself will be on a raft.

But we won't machine-gun you. We weren't brought up that way. No, we'll give you a little taste of what it's like in the salt water. Aircraft from the Fleet Air Arm will catch up with you, they'll dive-bomb you, wave after wave after wave, and your guns will be as useless as ours was. And a battleship will come up, and I hope it's the *Warspite,* and you'll be shattered. You'll see your bridge go up in flames, as ours did. You'll see your mates hanging round on the decks, the same as I did. You'll see your ship sink, as I did. And you'll be there in the water, struggling as we were, and your life-jacket won't hold you up, and you'll go down and down and down, and the water will come in your eyes and your ears, and down your mouth, and you'll see death in front of you. And you'll come up to the surface, and the British seamen will get hold of you, and will drag you on board the boat. Because we don't leave men to drown.

But, remember, Mr. Raider, that when we have finished with you—and we won't use blackjacks[64] or castor oil[65]—you'll wish, and you'll hope, and you'll pray that you had been left to drown, as you left us. But we didn't drown.

Your day is coming. Look out for it.

---

64 [A cosh or bludgeon.]
65 [This was a punishment by Mussolini's Blackshirts. The victim would be force-fed the oil and then suffer painful diarrhoea, and perhaps even die from the resulting dehydration. The fascists would say that their power was backed by "the bludgeon and castor oil".]

14. Sister Morris

I WAS ON A HOSPITAL ship. I had got over the worst. They amputated my leg, I had got over my pneumonia, I was recovering.

When suddenly, out of the night, and out of the dark, my own self came up, and, if you can put it that way, tried to get me down.

I remember one night, as I lay in my bed there, the lights had just gone out and the boys who were with me were tossing and turning and had settled down into an uneasy slumber. And as I lay there came the slap, slap, slap, of the waves outside.

Suddenly, a vision came to me. A vision who for me would for ever walk the streets of my home town—on one leg and with two crutches. The vision of a man who would not be young and strong and fit, but a cripple. A dreadful, awful, horrible thing to happen to anybody.

I remember laying back in bed and sweating at the thought of it. Just to think—no more dances, no more walks, no more horse riding, no more swimming. One leg, and two crutches.

Despite all I had ever been through, I felt, at last my misfortunes were coming to a head, and I was going under.

And I wasn't alone. In the next bed to me, was a little porter from Covent Garden.[66] He was wounded as badly as I was. In the bed in front of me was little Ben from Rochdale, wounded much worse than I was. His first trip as ordinary seaman, he lay there, and worried about his mother and his father; worried about his life, for he, too, had lost a leg.

And I remember the shades of misery and unhappiness were coming over me, when Sister Morris, our Ward Sister,

---

66 [At the time, Covent Garden was the main fruit and vegetable wholesale market in London.]

came round on her nightly inspection. And as she passed my bed I remember I put my hand out and grabbed hold of her. She said, "What is wrong?" And I remember ever so distinctly saying, "Sister, do you think that any girl would ever fall in love with me—with one leg?" And I remember her looking at me, with a torch shining on her white breast, and she said, "Of course they will. I think I could".

And remembering that and remembering her voice I fell asleep.

I was there, and Charlie and Bert and the whole ward was full of us. The whole ward was full of us and Sister Morris gave me that message.

I shall never forget her, and Sister, if you're listening I have a message for you. I did find her, and she did.

I met her not so long ago. I have two feet now and I can dance and I can play tennis and in another month I'll be going back to sea.

15. My Street

YOU ALL KNOW YOUR street, the street where you were born. In my case, I was born in this particular house in this particular street. I had lived there all my life, and I had sailed from there as a sailor, and it was pretty dreadful to come home because my particular home town had received—shall we say *attention* from the Hun; and I didn't know what to expect. But all the time when I was coming home I kept thinking of Egerton Street,[67] where I was born—my mother and my father, and when you come down the front garden and look down the road, and at the bottom there you find our lifeboat, the *William and Kate Johnstone*,[68] and you see the docks and you know everybody.

I remember coming home so well, when they met me at the station, with a car and ran me home, and I saw damage of various descriptions. I saw houses with their windows out, and my heart was in my mouth until that car—it was a tiny little one—came hurtling round the corner, and there was No. 57 and it was absolutely all right. Mother was there at the door, and I remember getting out of the car and going over to meet her, very stiffly and ungainly because I had gone away with two shoes and socks, and I came back with one.

When mother saw me, she didn't cry. We don't cry in my family. We merely shook hands, and she kissed me and said, "I'm glad to see you home". And across the road there came all the neighbours. "Hullo, Frank, how are you? I'm so glad to see you back." All of them, everybody that I knew.

There into my own little front room—they'd even put my bed down there, so that I could sleep quietly and comforta-

---

67 [This is in New Brighton, Wallasey. The Mersey is visible from the end of the street.]
68 [In service from 1923 to 1950. A Barnett-class lifeboat, which, when launched, was the largest lifeboat in the world at 18 metres long. The boat has been preserved and is a charter boat presently moored at Ramsgate.]

bly and wouldn't have any stairs to climb. That homecoming I'll remember. Oh, to come home from anything else would have been an anti-climax, but to come back to Egerton Street as a wounded sailor! That was something.

Let me tell you about this street. At the bottom, as I said, is our lifeboat, she's only saved a matter of about seven hundred and fifty lives in this war, just seven hundred and fifty lives. All the lifeboat crew live just close to me. At the very bottom of the road, on the right-hand side, there lives a young gentleman who last attained fame by doing a trip on the *Altmark*.[69] You never see him now. He came out of the *Altmark* and went back to oil tankers. He said it was a lot safer. He comes home about every four months for about thirty-six hours, and then goes away again. And then next door to him there is a laddie who has had about four certificates from the National Lifeboat affair for rescues at sea. He is a lifeboat man, also a local fisherman. His family have lived in my little home town for about three hundred years. I'd like you to meet him some time or other.

And then next door to me there is a little laddie, Able Seaman. His first name is Mickey—very, very sunburnt, and with startlingly blue eyes, like the sky looking through the eyes of a skull almost. Because that's how he looked when I saw him the last time. He'd had ten days in an open boat, but of course Mickey's gone back to sea, he'd had about seven days at home and couldn't stand it.

And then further up, George—my friend George. George went down on the *Courageous*. Further up than him we had our wildest spark, Billy who was with me down on the *Silver Foam*,[70] when we were on the beach on that glorious summer of 1938—when we had all the mill girls and all the trippers coming down. Piling them into the boat, and running them up and down the river. Heavenly times!—One shilling for adults, sixpence for children, with everybody getting seasick,

---

69 [See page 68.]
70 [See page 69.]

and roars of laughter resounding all over the river. Bill was the life and soul of the *Silver Foam,* but Bill was blown up on a mine sweeper.

Further up at the top we have Stanley. Stanley came home, so Mother told me, about nine months ago and said nothing to anyone, and then he pushed off back to sea. And then about a month after that she opened a newspaper, and found that some enterprising reporter had got hold of the story of Stanley. Stanley, it appeared, was a gun-layer[71] on board an oil tanker, and about 500 east[72] of Trinidad he was on the poop one morning when a German submarine came to the surface, about 800 yards dead astern.

Stanley was a very, very wise laddie—he had his gun already loaded. He merely walked quietly towards the trigger; depressed the gun; put on his elevation; got his sights across the conning tower—and let fly.

The submarine disappeared in a cloud of smoke, and later large patches of oil were seen, and several very disconsolate Huns were brought on board and were given er—well, they were made very welcome.

All those people live in my street. Good people, so kindhearted. So honest and so gentle. Men with the deep sea in their eyes, men who have lived in the sight of God and man. Decent, clean, honourable lives. Men who you could imagine standing on the decks of the *Revenge*[73] with Sir Richard Grenville. Men who you know were on the *Victory*[74] with Nelson at Trafalgar. Two who I know were on the *Exeter*[75]— from my street, my little Egerton Street. But I was thinking, it could be your street, as well as my street. Shall we say it's *our* street, Victory Street. I think you'll all agree that it is.

---

71 [The person who aims the gun.]
72 [Presumably 500 nautical miles, which is nearly 1000 km: this would be towards the centre of the southern part of the North Atlantic Ocean.]
73 [See page 69.]
74 [See page 70.]
75 [See page 71.]

Postscript

As this book was going to press, Frank went back to sea as a seaman gunner.

He took with him a letter of appreciation from the Minister of Information,[76] who had heard some of his talks.

---

76 [The Ministry of information was created during the First World War and then brought back for the Second. The role of this department was publicity for the war effort and propaganda.]

Appendix

Details of the vessels mentioned in this book

SS *British Corporal*

SS[77] *British Corporal* was a 6,972 gross register tonnage[78] tanker that was built in 1922 by Palmers Shipbuilding & Iron Co., Jarrow. She was built for the British Tanker Company (BTC).

BTC was the maritime transport arm of the Anglo-Persian Oil Co., the forerunner of British Petroleum (BP). Formed in 1915, with an initial fleet of seven oil tankers, the BTC became the BP Tanker Company in 1955.

The incident that Laskier mentions happened at 05.15 on 6 August 1937. *British Corporal* was attacked by three Spanish Nationalist aircraft when she was 30 nautical miles (56 km) west of Algiers while on a voyage from Abadan, Iran, to Avonmouth (Bristol) with a cargo of petrol. The raid lasted an hour, with bombs and machine guns being used. *British Corporal* was only slightly damaged, with her radio being put out of action for a time. None of the crew of *British Corporal* were injured. Following the incident, she put into Algiers.[79]

In 1940, the ship was damaged in an attack by German E-boats. E-boat was the Allied forces' official description of the German navy's S-boot or *Schnellboot*. This was a small boat, armed with torpedoes and guns, which was capable of reaching 48 knots (89 km/h).

---

77 [Single-screw steamship; meaning the ship had one propeller.]
78 [The total internal volume of a ship in register tons. Register tons are equal to 100 cubic feet (~3 cubic metres).]
79 [A port and the capital city of Algeria. At the time it was a colony of France.]

British Corporal was transferred to the British Ministry of War Transport and renamed *Empire Corporal*. She returned to service in 1942 following repairs, but was torpedoed and sunk on 18 August by *U-598*[80] off of the coast of Cuba with the loss of six of her crew of 55.

SS *City of Benares*

This was a steam passenger ship built for Ellerman Lines in Glasgow. She was launched on 5 August 1935, and completed in October 1936. *City of Benares* was powered by three steam turbines which gave her a speed of 15 knots (28 km/h).

During the Second World War the *City of Benares* was used as an evacuee ship to transport 90 children from war-torn Britain to the safety of Canada. The ship was torpedoed in September 1940 by the German submarine *U-48* with a heavy loss of life, including the death of 77 of the evacuated children. The sinking caused such a shock in Britain that it led to the government cancelling its plans to relocate British children abroad.

MV *San Demetrio*

This was one of several motor tankers of about 8,000 gross register tonnage built for Eagle Oil & Shipping in the later 1930s. She was built by the Blythswood Shipbuilding Co. of Glasgow.

MV[81] *San Demetrio* had loaded 11,200 tons of aviation fuel in Galveston, Texas and was bound for Avonmouth (Bristol). She was one of 38 ships that joined a convoy for the passage across the North Atlantic and left Halifax, Nova Scotia

---

80 [German naval submarines were numbered not named. U-boat is an anglicised version of the German word *U-Boot*, a shortening of *Unterseeboot* ("under-the-sea boat"). *U-598* was sunk by US aircraft off of the Brazilian coast in 1943.]
81 [Motor vessel.]

Appendix

on 28 October 1940. The destroyers HMCS[82] *Columbia* and HMCS *St. Francis* escorted the convoy out of Canadian home waters but once clear of the coast, the convoy's sole escort was the armed merchant cruiser HMS[83] *Jervis Bay* (see entry, page 65) – a converted passenger liner that had been armed with seven outdated BL 6-inch Mk VII naval guns and a pair of 3-inch anti-aircraft guns.

On 5 November 1940, the German cruiser *Admiral Scheer* (see entry, page 66) found the convoy and attacked. Captain Fegen of HMS *Jervis Bay* steamed out towards the raider so as to delay *Admiral Scheer* and to allow the convoy to scatter and escape. *Jervis Bay* was completely outclassed, but she fought for 22 minutes before she was sunk with the loss of 190 of her crew.

The *Admiral Scheer* hit *San Demetrio* with several shells. Despite the exploding shells and the resultant fire, the ship's highly flammable cargo did not explode. Nevertheless, it was believed that the fire could cause the aviation fuel to blow up so it was decided to abandon ship. The crew escaped in two lifeboats while their ship remained under fire from *Admiral Scheer*.

At dawn on 7 November 1940, the *San Demetrio* was about five nautical miles (9 km) downwind so the crew set sailed towards her and re-boarded. Despite the damage and fire, only 200 tons of *San Demetrio*'s highly volatile cargo had been lost. There was only one fatality, John Boyle, who had been injured jumping into the lifeboat after the original battle and gradually began to feel unwell. He was propped up in the engine room, to watch the gauges, but died of a haemorrhage after two days.

---

82 [His Majesty's Canadian Ship.]
83 [His Majesty's Ship (or Her Majesty's Ship) was first used in its abbreviated form for HMS *Phoenix* in 1783.]

The ship was the subject of a 1943 feature film, *San Demetrio London*, one of the few films that recognised the heroism of merchant navy crews during the Second World War.

SS *Eurylochus*

This was a 5,273 gross register tonnage steam-powered British freighter launched in 1913, built in Glasgow by the London & Glasgow Engineering & Iron Shipbuilding Co. and owned by the China Mutual Steam Navigation Co. of Liverpool.

On 29 January 1941, lookouts aboard the German auxiliary cruiser *Kormoran* spotted the merchant ship sailing without lights off of the coast of Sierra Leone. On approaching the vessel, *Kormoran* opened fire; her first salvo missed, but within minutes, the target was heavily damaged and aflame. It was suspected that other German warships had joined in the firing. The ship transmitted a distress signal, which *Kormoran* was unable to jam completely, but this ceased as crew members started to abandon ship. The raider stopped firing, but resumed when the merchantman attempted another transmission, and shore stations responded. Captured communications intercepts and the codebooks revealed that the target's identity was the *Eurylochus*, with a cargo of bombers for the Gold Coast (present-day Ghana). These intercepts also indicated that the British Air Ministry was aware of the attack, prompting the *Kormoran* to sink the *Eurylochus*. This was accomplished with a single torpedo.

Thirty-nine Chinese and four British crew were recovered by the Germans before the *Kormoran* fled the area with British warships *Norfolk* and *Devonshire* in pursuit. Another 28 survivors were found by the Spanish merchant ship *Monte Tiede* later that night, with ten men killed during the attack or lost at sea. Among the rescued was Frank Laskier, the ship's gunner.

Appendix

HMS *Jervis Bay*

This was a 14,164 gross register tonnage steam-powered British liner launched in 1922 as SS *Jervis Bay* and built by Vickers Ltd in Barrow-in-Furness.

The ship was acquired by the Royal Navy in 1939 and was used as a convoy escort during the Second World War. It was armed with seven 6-inch guns dating back to 1898 and two 3-inch guns of 1894 design.

In May 1940, while escorting a convoy of 37 merchant ships from Bermuda and Halifax to Britain, *Jervis Bay* encountered the German warship *Admiral Scheer* (see entry, page 66) about 755 nautical miles (1,398 km) south of Iceland. The captain of the *Jervis Bay*, Edward Fegen, ordered the convoy to scatter, and set his own ship on a course towards the German warship to draw its fire. *Jervis Bay* was hopelessly outgunned and out-ranged by the 11-inch guns of the German ship, but she attacked the larger ship nonetheless, firing more to distract the German ship from the merchantmen than with hopes of doing any real damage. Although the German's shells ravaged the *Jervis Bay*, wounding Fegen and killing many of those on board, Fegen and the surviving crew fought on until their ship was sunk. Captain Fegen, and many of the ship's company, went down with their vessel. Fegen received a posthumous Victoria Cross for his bravery.

HMS *Courageous*

This ship was the first of the Courageous-class cruisers commissioned by the Royal Navy during the First World War. It was built by Armstrong Whitworth in Newcastle upon Tyne and launched in 1916. Powered by four steam turbines, she had a maximum speed of 30 knots (56 km/h).

Courageous was decommissioned after the First World War and then rebuilt as an aircraft carrier during the mid-1920s.

On the evening of 3 September 1939, *Courageous* departed Plymouth for an anti-submarine patrol in the Western Approaches, escorted by four destroyers. On the evening of 17 September 1939, she was on one such patrol off the coast of Ireland. Two of the four destroyers escorting her had been sent to help a merchant ship under attack and all her aircraft had returned from patrols. During this time, *Courageous* was stalked for over two hours by *U-29*. The carrier then turned into the wind to launch her aircraft. This put the ship right across the bow of the submarine, which fired three torpedoes. Two of the torpedoes struck the ship on her port side before any aircraft took off, knocking out all electrical power, and she capsized, sinking in 20 minutes with the loss of 519 of her crew, including her captain. The survivors were rescued by the Dutch ocean liner *Veendam* and the British freighter *Collingworth*. The two escorting destroyers counter-attacked *U-29* for four hours, but the submarine escaped.

Courageous was the first British warship to be sunk by German forces. The commander of the German submarine force, Commodore Karl Dönitz, regarded the sinking of *Courageous* as "a wonderful success" and it led to widespread jubilation in the German navy.

Admiral Scheer

This was an armoured cruiser (often termed a pocket battleship by the British) which served with the German navy during the Second World War. She was built at the Reichsmarinewerft shipyard in Wilhelmshaven and launched in November 1934.

The ship was nominally under the 10,000-ton limitation on warship size imposed by the Treaty of Versailles, although with a full load displacement of 15,180 tons, she significantly exceeded it. The Treaty of Versailles marked the end of the First World War and placed restrictions on Germany's military capabilities in the misguided hope that it would prevent future German aggression.

Armed with six 11-inch guns and with a top speed of 28 knots (52 km/h), *Admiral Scheer* outclassed all but a handful of ships in the British and French navies.

Admiral Scheer saw heavy service including a deployment to Spain during the Spanish Civil War, where she bombarded the port of Almería in south-east Spain. Her first operation during the Second World War was a commerce-raiding[84] operation in the southern Atlantic Ocean. During her service, she sank 113,223 gross register tons of shipping, making her the most successful surface raider of the war. Following her return to Germany, she was deployed to northern Norway to discourage shipping to the Soviet Union.

After returning to Germany at the end of 1942, the vessel served as a training ship until the end of 1944, when she was used to support ground operations against the Soviet army. She moved to Kiel for repairs in March 1945, where she was capsized by RAF bombers in a raid on 9 April 1945 and partially scrapped.

HMS *Warspite*

This battleship was built for the Royal Navy during the early 1910s and completed during the First World War in 1915. When she was launched, the use of oil as a fuel was untried and her 15-inch guns were revolutionary concepts in the naval arms race between Britain and Germany.

During the Second World War, *Warspite* was involved in the Norwegian campaign in early 1940 and was transferred to the Mediterranean later that year where the ship participated in fleet actions against the Italian navy while also escorting convoys and bombarding Italian troops ashore.

---

84 [Commerce raiding is the disrupting of supply chains by attacking merchant shipping.]

She was damaged by German aircraft during the Battle of Crete in mid-1941 and required six months of repairs in the USA. They were completed after the start of the Pacific War in December and the ship sailed across the Pacific to join the Eastern Fleet in the Indian Ocean in early 1942. *Warspite* returned home in mid-1943 to conduct naval gunfire support as part of the Italian campaign. She was badly damaged by German radio-controlled glider bombs during the landings at Salerno and spent most of the next year under repair. The ship bombarded German positions during the D-Day landings and the Anglo-Canadian attack to open the port of Antwerp in Belgium in 1944, despite not being fully repaired. These actions earned her the most battle honours ever awarded to an individual ship in the Royal Navy.

Decommissioned in 1945, *Warspite* ran aground while under tow in 1947 on rocks near Prussia Cove, Cornwall, and was eventually broken up nearby.

Altmark

This was a German oil tanker and supply vessel, one of five built between 1937 and 1939 by Howaldtswerke in Kiel, northern Germany. She was launched in 1937 and had a displacement of 21,000 tons. She is best known for her support of the German commerce raider *Admiral Graf Spee*.

Altmark was assigned to support *Admiral Graf Spee* during her raid in the South Atlantic between September and December 1939. British seamen rescued from the ships sunk by *Admiral Graf Spee* were transferred to *Altmark*.

After the *Admiral Graf Spee* had been heavily damaged by British cruisers in the Battle of the River Plate, and subsequently scuttled by her crew in December 1939, the *Altmark* attempted to return to Germany alone, steaming around the north of Britain and then towards Norway, which was neutral at the time.

Appendix

On 14 February 1940, *Altmark*, proceeding south within Norwegian territorial waters, was discovered by three British Lockheed Hudson aircraft from RAF Thornaby (near Middlesbrough) and pursued by several British destroyers led by HMS *Cossack*. Late on 16 February 1940, she was fired on while the Norwegian navy stood by and took no action save for raising a protest flag. The German tanker was then boarded by a party from the *Cossack*. During an attempted escape across the ice, seven of the *Altmark* crew were shot and in the skirmish the *Altmark* was run aground. The British had intended to tow the ship back to a Scottish port, but the damage to the tanker's stern made this impossible. The British prisoners on the *Altmark* were rescued and released.

Silver Foam

This vessel is listed in the Admiralty's 1944 "Red List" of "Minor War Vessels in Home Waters" as being a naval auxiliary boat based in Greenock Pool, Clyde area of the Western Approaches.

The Association of Little Ships, which has a list of vessels know to have participated in the Dunkirk evacuation ("Operation Dynamo") of 1940, lists *Silver Foam* as being involved at Dynamo beach.

Laskier describes the boat during peace time and it seems to be a small boat working on the Mersey. Sadly, we have been unable to trace any further information.

Revenge

This was an English race-built galleon[85] of 46 guns, built in 1577 and captured by the Spanish in 1591, sinking soon

---

85 [Typically square-rigged sailing ships with three or more decks and masts. The name is thought to come from the Spanish *galeón*, meaning "armed merchant ship".]

afterwards. She was the first of thirteen English and Royal Navy ships to bear the name.

Revenge came to her end in a bizarre episode that has become a legend. In order to impede a Spanish naval recovery after the Armada,[86] Queen Elizabeth I's Treasurer of the Navy, Sir John Hawkins, proposed a blockade to intercept the ships bringing treasure to Spain from its empire in the Americas. *Revenge* was on such a patrol in the summer of 1591 under the command of Sir Richard Grenville, when they encountered the Spanish and were reported to be "out-gunned, out-fought, and out-numbered fifty-three to one", and when the end looked certain, Grenville ordered the *Revenge* to be sunk. This led, years later, to the Victorian-era poet Alfred, Lord Tennyson, to proclaim in "'The Revenge': A Ballad of the Fleet" *"Sink me the ship, Master Gunner—sink her, split her in twain! Fall into the hands of God, not into the hands of Spain!"* Grenville's officers could not go along with this order (*"And the gunner said, 'Ay, ay,' but the seamen made reply: 'We have children, we have wives'"*) and a surrender was agreed by which the lives of the officers and crew would be spared. After an assurance of proper conduct, and having held off dozens of Spanish ships, *Revenge* at last surrendered. The injured Grenville died of wounds two days later aboard the Spanish flagship.[87] However, the captured but heavily damaged *Revenge* never reached Spain, but was lost along with a large number of the Spanish vessels in a storm off of the Azores.

HMS *Victory*

A 104-gun first-rate ship of the line of the Royal Navy, ordered in 1758, laid down in 1759 and launched in 1765.

---

86 [The Portuguese or Spanish word for a naval fleet, however in this sense is means the Spanish fleet's abortive attempt to invade England in 1588.]
87 [The flagship is the ship in a fleet that carries the commanding admiral.]

Appendix

She is best known for her role as Lord Nelson's flagship at the Battle of Trafalgar on 21 October 1805.

In 1922, she was moved to a dry dock at Portsmouth and preserved as a museum ship. She has been the flagship of the First Sea Lord since October 2012 and is the world's oldest naval ship still in commission, with over 240 years' service.

HMS *Exeter*

This was the second and last *York*-class heavy cruiser built for the Royal Navy in Devonport Dockyard, Plymouth and launched in 1929. She spent most of the 1930s assigned to the Atlantic Fleet or the North America and West Indies Station. When the Second World War began in September 1939, the cruiser was assigned to patrol South American waters against German commerce raiders. *Exeter* was one of three British cruisers that fought the *Admiral Graf Spee* later that year in the Battle of the River Plate. She was severely damaged during the battle, and in the shipyard for over a year.

After her repairs were completed, the ship spent most of 1941 on convoy escort duties before she was transferred to the Far East following the start of the Pacific War in December. *Exeter* was generally assigned to escorting convoys to and from Singapore during the Malayan Campaign, and she continued on those duties in early February 1942 as the Japanese prepared to invade the Dutch East Indies.

Exeter was damaged early in the Battle of the Java Sea in 1942, and had to withdraw. Two days later, she attempted to escape approaching Japanese forces, but she was intercepted and sunk by Japanese ships in the Second Battle of the Java Sea.

Most of her crewmen survived the sinking and were rescued by the Japanese navy. Subsequently, about a quarter of them died during Japanese captivity. *Exeter*'s wreck was discovered in early 2007 and it was declared a war grave.

www.ingramcontent.com/pod-product-compliance
Lightning Source LLC
Chambersburg PA
CBHW071755080526
44588CB00013B/2250